Je

by Iain Gray

Lang**Syne**

PUBLISHING

WRITING *to* REMEMBER

LangSyne
PUBLISHING
WRITING *to* REMEMBER

79 Main Street, Newtongrange,
Midlothian EH22 4NA
Tel: 0131 344 0414   Fax: 0845 075 6085
E-mail: info@lang-syne.co.uk
www.langsyneshop.co.uk

Design by Dorothy Meikle
Printed by Printwell Ltd
© Lang Syne Publishers Ltd 2018

ISBN 978-1-85217-521-4

Jenkins

MOTTO:
Advance but cautiously.

CREST:
A lion passant atop a coronet.

NAME variations include:
Jenkin
Jenkinson
Jenkyns

Chapter one:

The origins of popular surnames

by George Forbes and Iain Gray

If you don't know where you came from, you won't know where you're going is a frequently quoted observation and one that has a particular resonance today when there has been a marked upsurge in interest in genealogy, with increasing numbers of people curious to trace their family roots.

Main sources for genealogical research include census returns and official records of births, marriages and deaths – and the key to unlocking the detail they contain is obviously a family surname, one that has been 'inherited' and passed from generation to generation.

No matter our station in life, we all have a surname – but it was not until about the middle of the fourteenth century that the practice of being identified by a particular surname became commonly established throughout the British Isles.

Previous to this, it was normal for a person to be identified through the use of only a forename.

But as population gradually increased and there were many more people with the same forename, surnames were adopted to distinguish one person, or community, from another.

Many common English surnames are patronymic in origin, meaning they stem from the forename of one's father – with 'Johnson,' for example, indicating 'son of John.'

It was the Normans, in the wake of their eleventh century conquest of Anglo-Saxon England, a pivotal moment in the nation's history, who first brought surnames into usage – although it was a gradual process.

For the Normans, these were names initially based on the title of their estates, local villages and chateaux in France to distinguish and identify these landholdings.

Such grand descriptions also helped enhance the prestige of these warlords and generally glorify their lofty positions high above the humble serfs slaving away below in the pecking order who had only single names, often with Biblical connotations as in Pierre and Jacques.

The only descriptive distinctions among the peasantry concerned their occupations, like 'Pierre the swineherd' or 'Jacques the ferryman.'

Roots of surnames that came into usage in England not only included Norman-French, but also Old French, Old Norse, Old English, Middle English, German, Latin, Greek, Hebrew and the Gaelic languages of the Celts.

The Normans themselves were originally Vikings, or 'Northmen', who raided, colonised and eventually settled down around the French coastline.

The had sailed up the Seine in their longboats in 900AD under their ferocious leader Rollo and ruled the roost in north eastern France before sailing over to conquer England in 1066 under Duke William of Normandy – better known to posterity as William the Conqueror, or King William I of England.

Granted lands in the newly-conquered England, some of their descendants later acquired territories in Wales, Scotland and Ireland – taking not only their own surnames, but also the practice of adopting a surname, with them.

But it was in England where Norman rule and custom first impacted, particularly in relation to the adoption of surnames.

This is reflected in the famous *Domesday Book*, a massive survey of much of England and Wales, ordered by William I, to determine who owned what, what it was worth and therefore how much they were liable to pay in taxes to the voracious Royal Exchequer.

Completed in 1086 and now held in the National Archives in Kew, London, 'Domesday' was an Old English word meaning 'Day of Judgement.'

This was because, in the words of one contemporary chronicler, "its decisions, like those of the Last Judgement, are unalterable."

It had been a requirement of all those English landholders – from the richest to the poorest – that they identify themselves for the purposes of the survey and for future reference by means of a surname.

This is why the *Domesday Book*, although written in Latin as was the practice for several centuries with both civic and ecclesiastical records, is an invaluable source for the early appearance of a wide range of English surnames.

Several of these names were coined in connection with occupations.

These include Baker and Smith, while Cooks, Chamberlains, Constables and Porters were to be found carrying out duties in large medieval households.

The church's influence can be found in names such as Bishop, Friar and Monk while the popular name of Bennett derives from the late fifth to mid-sixth century Saint Benedict, founder of the Benedictine order of monks.

The early medical profession is represented by Barber, while businessmen produced names that include Merchant and Sellers.

Down at the village watermill, the names that cropped up included Millar/Miller, Walker and Fuller, while other self-explanatory trades included Cooper, Tailor, Mason and Wright.

Even the scenery was utilised as in Moor, Hill, Wood and Forrest – while the hunt and the chase supplied names that include Hunter, Falconer, Fowler and Fox.

Colours are also a source of popular surnames, as in Black, Brown, Gray/Grey, Green and White, and would have denoted the colour of the clothing the person habitually wore or, apart from the obvious exception of 'Green', one's hair colouring or even complexion.

The surname Red developed into Reid, while

Blue was rare and no-one wanted to be associated with yellow.

Rather self-important individuals took surnames that include Goodman and Wiseman, while physical attributes crept into surnames such as Small and Little.

Many families proudly boast the heraldic device known as a Coat of Arms, as featured on our front cover.

The central motif of the Coat of Arms would originally have been what was borne on the shield of a warrior to distinguish himself from others on the battlefield.

Not featured on the Coat of Arms, but highlighted on page three, is the family motto and related crest – with the latter frequently different from the central motif.

Adding further variety to the rich cultural heritage that is represented by surnames is the appearance in recent times in lists of the 100 most common names found in England of ones that include Khan, Patel and Singh – names that have proud roots in the vast sub-continent of India.

Echoes of a far distant past can still be found in our surnames and they can be borne with pride in commemoration of our forebears.

Chapter two:

Ancient roots

**A surname that is popular throughout the length
and breadth of the British Isles, 'Jenkins' is
nevertheless particularly identified with Wales.**

It derives from what were the personal names
'Jan' 'Jen' and 'Jon', more commonly rendered as
'John'.

The surname therefore means either 'son of
John' or 'little John', while the 'kin' element is of
Dutch origin, and was first introduced by Flemish
settlers in the twelfth century.

In common with many other surnames, it
was popularised in the wake of the Norman Conquest
of 1066, but many of those who would later adopt
it as a name were present from a much earlier
period.

Earliest written records of the name appear in
what is now the modern-day English county of
Sussex, while large concentrations of its bearers were
also found in the Devon and Cornwall areas.

The name is also recorded in Monmouthshire,
Wales, and this indicates that some of its bearers today

may be of either original Welsh roots or English, Anglo-Saxon roots.

For those bearers of Welsh origin, flowing through their veins may well be the blood of the ancient Britons.

Of Celtic pedigree, these early inhabitants of the British Isles were settled for centuries from a line south of the River Forth in Scotland all the way down to the south coast of England and with a particular presence in Wales.

Speaking a Celtic language known as Brythonic, they boasted a glorious culture that flourished even after the Roman invasion of Britain in 43 AD and the subsequent consolidation of Roman power by about 84 AD.

With many of the original Britons absorbing aspects of Roman culture, they became 'Romano-British' – while still retaining their own proud Celtic heritage.

Following the withdrawal of the last Roman legions from Britain in 406, what is now modern-day Wales, or *Cymru*, fragmented into a number of independent kingdoms – with the most powerful king being recognised as overall ruler.

Recognised as King of the Britons, he had to

battle with not only internal rivals but also the depredations of the wild sea rovers known as the Vikings, or Northmen.

There were in addition the Anglo-Saxons, also early ancestors of bearers of the Jenkins name, to contend with.

These were those Germanic tribes who invaded and settled in the south and east of the island of Britain from about the early fifth century.

They were composed of the Jutes, from the area of the Jutland Peninsula in modern Denmark, the Saxons from Lower Saxony, in modern Germany and the Angles from the Angeln area of Germany.

It was the Angles who gave the name 'Engla land', or 'Aengla land' – better known as 'England.'

The Anglo-Saxons held sway in what became England from approximately 550 to 1066, with the main kingdoms those of Sussex, Wessex, Northumbria, Mercia, Kent, East Anglia and Essex.

Whoever controlled the most powerful of these kingdoms was tacitly recognised as overall 'king' – one of the most noted being Alfred the Great, King of Wessex from 871 to 899.

The Anglo-Saxons, meanwhile, had usurped the power of the indigenous Britons, such as those found in Wales, and who referred to them as 'Saeson' or 'Saxones.'

It is from this that the Scottish Gaelic term for 'English people' of 'Sasannach' derives, the Irish Gaelic 'Sasanach' and the Welsh 'Saeson.'

The death knell of Anglo-Saxon supremacy and also what remained of Welsh independence was sounded with the Norman Conquest and the defeat of Harold II, the last of the Anglo-Saxon monarchs, at the battle of Hastings.

Within an astonishingly short space of time, Norman manners, customs and law were imposed on England – laying the basis for what subsequently became established 'English' custom and practice.

In 1282, by which time most of Wales had come under Anglo-Norman rule, final rebellion against this was crushed by England's Edward I, and it is from this date that the heir apparent to the British throne has borne the title of Prince of Wales.

An abortive rebellion was led in the early fifteenth century by the freedom fighter Owain Glyndŵr, while in the following century, under Henry VIII, Wales was 'incorporated' into the English kingdom; in 1707, in common with Scotland, Wales became part of the United Kingdom.

The Jenkins name is one that features prominently in the historical record.

Although very little is known with certainty concerning his background, including even his date of birth and year of death, Thomas Jenkins is famed for having been the headmaster of the young William Shakespeare, who was born in 1564.

It is known that from 1575 to 1579, Jenkins was the headmaster of the King Edward VI Grammar School in Stratford-upon-Avon, while some sources assert he was of Welsh roots.

As headmaster, he would undoubtedly have been in charge of the education of the future playwright and dramatist, who is known to have been a pupil at the school.

Shakespeare, in common with other great literary figures, absorbed elements of his own life and times for inspiration for his work, and it is perhaps no coincidence that his play *The Merry Wives of Windsor* features a Welsh schoolmaster, Sir David Evans.

Teaching Shakespeare Latin and grammar, it is said that Jenkins was also responsible for stirring his interest in the colourful legendary history of the British Isles – a fascination with the dim and distant historical past that is reflected in plays such as *Cymbeline* and *King Lear*.

There has been much academic speculation over the years as to Thomas Jenkins' background.

The Shakespearian scholar M.C. Bradbrook, in his 1978 *Shakespeare: The Poet in his World* asserts that the available evidence points to Jenkins not having been born in Wales but in London.

His father, according to the scholar, was a servant to Sir Thomas White, who had founded the Merchant Taylors' School in London and St John's College, Oxford.

Through his father's association with Sir Thomas, Bradbrook claims, Jenkins was able to attend the school and also later graduate from St John's College.

He also interestingly states that while at school he would have been taught by Richard Mulcaster, author of the *Elementaire* and an advocate of teaching through play-acting.

It is perhaps through this, via Jenkins, via Mulcaster that Shakespeare's love of the stage was fostered.

Chapter three:

High seas and politics

One bearer of the Jenkins name with a particularly unusual claim to historical fame was the British master mariner Robert Jenkins – responsible for sparking off a war between Britain and Spain – colourfully known as The War of Jenkins' Ear – that lasted from 1739 to 1748.

His date of birth is not clear, but it is known that he was born in Llanelli, Wales.

It was while returning to English shores from the West Indies in command of the brig *Rebecca* that in April of 1731 his vessel was stopped and boarded by the Spanish ship *Isabella* on suspicion of smuggling.

The *Isabella's* commander, Captain Leon Fandino, ordered that Jenkins be tied to a mast and then, drawing his sword, deftly sliced off his left ear.

He was then reputed to have told Jenkins, before allowing him to continue on his way, to tell his king, George II: "The same will happen to him if caught doing the same", i.e. smuggling.

Arriving in England in early June, Jenkins

briefed the king on the incident and submitted a sworn deposition to the Duke of Newcastle, Secretary for the Colonies.

He stated that the Spanish commander had: "... taken hold of his left ear and with his cutlass slit it down, and then another of the Spaniards took hold of it and tore it off, but gave him the piece of his ear again."

A report on Jenkins' ordeal was then forwarded to the British Commander-in-Chief in the West Indies, who then lodged an official complaint with the Spanish governor of Havana.

No further action was taken, but patriotic public passions were aroused when a greatly exaggerated account appeared in *The Gentleman's Magazine*.

It indignantly stated that the crew of the *Rebecca* were "put to the torture, part of which was that they hanged up the Captain three times, once with the cabin-boy at his feet; they then cut off one of his ears, took away his candles and other instruments, and detained him a whole day."

But it was not until seven years later, in the spring of 1738 and by which time British merchants were engaged in a trade war with their Spanish counterparts and looking for an excuse to go to actual war, that Jenkins was called upon again to give an account of the incident before a special committee of the House of Commons.

This he did, producing for added gruesome effect his severed ear, which was pickled in a jar.

The king was asked to seek formal redress from Spain and, when all diplomatic efforts failed, a formal declaration of naval warfare was declared by Britain in October of 1739.

Jenkins was given command of a ship in the service of the British East India Company and subsequently disappears from the historical record, while the inconclusive war that he had given his name to dragged on for another nine years.

One adventurous bearer of the name was the Welsh farmer, poet and diarist Joseph Jenkins who, when aged over 50, suddenly abandoned his wife and nine children for a new life in Australia.

Born in 1818 on a farm near Ystrad Aeron, in Ceredigion, and marrying in 1846, he bought the lease of Trecefal farm, Tregaron which, thanks to his industry and farming acumen, was judged in 1851 to be the best farm in the country, with Jenkins winning many prizes in agricultural shows.

With no proper formal education, he had embarked on a rigorous regime of self-education in addition to meticulously recording the details of his everyday life and observations, over a period of 58 years, in a series of diaries.

For reasons that remain unclear – although it may have been because of his almost insatiable thirst for knowledge and desire to widen his horizons beyond the agricultural landscape of Wales – he took off on his own for Australia, arriving at the port of Sandridge, Melbourne, in March of 1869.

Irregular employment followed, including gold prospecting and casual farm work in the area around the town of Castlemaine, while over a period of thirteen years he regularly won prizes for his Welsh verse skills at the St David's Day Eisteddfod held in Ballarat.

Later employed as a cleaner of streets and drains in the town of Maldon, at the age of 76 and after 25 years in Australia, he departed for his native land, arriving there in January of 1895.

On his return, and before his death four years later, he entrusted his precious collection of diaries to one of his daughters who stored them in the attic of her farmhouse.

They were not discovered until 70 years later, by his grand-daughter Francis Evans.

She, in turn, passed them to her uncle, the eminent London Harley Street cardiologist Dr William Evans, who edited and published them as *The Diary of a Welsh Swagman*.

Bearers of the Jenkins name have also stamped their mark on the world of politics and political activism.

Not only a prominent British Labour Party politician but also a leading light of CND – the Campaign for Nuclear Disarmament – Hugh Jenkins, Baron Jenkins of Putney, was born in 1908 in Enfield, Middlesex.

Serving during the Second World War with the Royal Observer Corps and then the RAF, at the end of the conflict he worked for a time on radio in Rangoon, Burma, as director of English programmes.

Back in Britain, he and his wife Marie became active in politics, joining in the opposition to the 1956 Suez War with Egypt and becoming active members of CND, formed in 1957.

Elected as Labour Member of Parliament (MP) for Putney in 1964, he was appointed Shadow

Arts Minister in 1963 and, from 1974 to 1976 served in the Labour Cabinet as Arts Minister.

He became chair of CND in 1978, the same year he lost his Parliamentary seat, and was made a life peer as Baron Jenkins of Putney two years later.

Serving as chair of CND until 1981 and then as vice-chair, it was during his tenure that the organisation underwent its major revival known as the 'Second Wave'; he died in 2004.

The son of a Welsh coal miner, Roy Jenkins was the highly influential politician born in 1920 in Abersychan, in one of the Jenkins' original heartlands of Monmouthshire.

The recipient of a first class honours degree in politics, philosophy and economics from Balliol College, Oxford he served during the Second World War with the Royal Artillery and then at the secret code-breaking centre at Bletchley Park, near Oxford.

Elected to the House of Commons as Labour MP for Southwark Central in 1948, and later representing Birmingham Stetchford after the Southwark Central constituency was abolished, he went on to serve in a number of high-level government posts.

These included Minister of Aviation and, from 1965 to 1967, Home Secretary – when a number of radical measures such as the effective abolition of capital punishment, legalisation of abortion, the relaxation of the divorce law and the decriminalisation of homosexuality were introduced.

Becoming disenchanted with what he perceived as the Labour Party's increasing swing to the left, he quit politics in 1976 and served as President of the European Commission from 1977 until 1981.

In 1981, along with fellow Labour Party moderates Dr David Owen, Shirley Williams and William Rodger, he founded the Social Democratic Party (SDP) – taking the seat of Glasgow Hillhead from the Conservatives in 1982.

Resigning as SDP leader in 1983, he later lost his seat to Labour, while the SDP later merged with the Liberal Party to form the Liberal Democrat Party.

Awarded a life peerage and in the late 1990s serving as an advisor to Labour Prime Minister Tony Blair and also chairing the Jenkins Commission on electoral reform, he died in 2003.

Born in 1926 in Port Talbot, Wales, David

Clive Jenkins, better known as Clive Jenkins, was the British trade union leader who, from 1969 to 1988, was general secretary of the white-collar union ASTMS – the Association of Scientific, Technical and Managerial Staffs.

Also chairman of the TUC – Trades Union Congress – from 1987 to 1988, his autobiography *All Against the Collar* was published nine years before his death in 1999.

Chapter four:

On the world stage

At one time the highest paid actor in Hollywood and known for his highly publicised and turbulent relationship with the actress Elizabeth Taylor, Richard Walter Jenkins was better known by his stage name of Richard Burton.

Born in 1925 in the small Welsh village of Pontrhydyfen, the son of a coal miner and the twelfth of thirteen children, it was through the encouragement of his teacher Philip H. Burton that he excelled in school drama productions.

It was in recognition of his teacher's early influence on him that he later adopted his surname.

Serving in the RAF from 1944 to 1949 as a navigator, he later signed for a theatrical agency in London and made his film debut in the 1949 film *The Last Days of Dolywn*.

Quickly becoming a major box office attraction, he starred in a number of notable films that include the 1952 *My Cousin Rachel*, the 1953 *The Rose*, the 1964 *Beckett*, the 1965 *The Spy Who Came in from the Cold*, the 1966 *Whose Afraid of*

Virginia Woolf? and the 1969 *Anne of the Thousand Days*.

All of these films won him Academy Award nominations as Best Actor, while other awards over his career include Tony Awards for Best Actor, a Golden Globe and a BAFTA.

He married fellow Hollywood star Elizabeth Taylor in 1964 and he became renowned for the expensive gifts of jewellery that he lavished on her.

They divorced in 1974 and remarried in 1975, but the relationship was at times so volatile – although they were deeply in love – that the marriage ended in divorce only nine months later.

Following the divorce, Burton explained their relationship by saying: "You can't keep clapping a couple of sticks of dynamite together without expecting them to blow up."

The recipient of a CBE, the Welsh actor died in 1984, while Elizabeth Taylor died in 2011.

Born in 1991 in Tampa, Florida, **Carter Jenkins** is the American actor who, in addition to television credits that include *CSI: Miami* and *CSI: New York*, has big screen credits that include the 2004 *Bad News Bears*, the 2006 *Keeping Up with the Steins* and, from 2009, *Aliens in the Attic*.

An American actor of stage, television and film, **Richard Jenkins** was born in 1947 in DeKalb, Illinois.

After working on stage with the Trinity Repertory Company in Providence, Rhode Island, he made his screen debut in the 1974 television movie *Feasting with Panthers*.

He is best known, however, for his role of Nathaniel Fisher in the television drama series *Six Feet Under*, for which he and fellow cast members received a Screen Actors Guild Award nomination in 2002 for Outstanding Performance by an Ensemble in a Drama Series.

Big screen credits include the 1985 *Silverado*, the 1999 *Outside Providence* and the 2008 *The Visitor* – for which he won a number of awards including a National Board of Review of Motion Pictures Spotlight Award.

Also on American shores, **Ken Jenkins**, born in 1940 in Dayton, Ohio is the veteran actor of television and film best known for his role of Dr Bob Kelso in the comedy series *Scrubs*. Other television credits include *The X-Files* and *Star Trek: The Next Generation*, while big screen credits include the 1998 remake of director Alfred Hitchcock's *Psycho*.

Behind the camera lens, **Chris Jenkins** is the American sound engineer who has worked on more than 150 films since 1979 and is the recipient of Academy Awards for Best Sound for the 1985 *Out of Africa* and, from 1992, *The Last of the Mohicans*.

He was also nominated for Academy Awards for his work on the 1990 *Dick Tracy* and the 2008 *Wanted*.

Bearers of the Jenkins name have also excelled in the highly competitive world of sport.

Born in New York in 1934, **Charlie Jenkins** is the American former athlete who was the recipient of two gold medals at the 1956 Olympics in Melbourne; these were for the 400-metres race and as a member of the winning U.S. 4x400-metres relay team.

His son Charles Jenkins, Jr., born in 1964, and better known as **Chip Jenkins**, is also an Olympic gold medallist – having been a member of the winning team in the 4x400-metres relay at the 1992 Olympics in Barcelona.

On the ice skating rink, **David Jenkins**, born in 1936 in Akron, Ohio is the American former figure skater who won the men's gold medal at the 1960 Winter Olympics.

In the boxing ring, **Lew Jenkins**, born in 1916

in Milburn, Texas, became lightweight champion of the world in May of 1940, holding the title until December of the following year.

Serving in the United States Coast Guard during the Second World War and the recipient of the Silver Star for his actions during the June 1944 Allied invasion of Normandy, he died in 1981.

In the rough and tumble that is the game of rugby union, **Neil Jenkins**, born in 1971 in Church Village, near Llantrisant is the Welsh former player who, in addition to playing for teams that include Pontypridd, Cardiff and Celtic Warriors, also played for the Wales national team and the British and Irish Lions.

The recipient of an MBE, at the time of writing he is ranked as Wales' highest ever points-scorer.

Born in 1895 in Llanelli, **Albert Jenkins** played club rugby for his home club between 1919 and 1928 in addition to earning 14 caps playing for his country between 1920 and 1928; he died in 1953.

From sport to the creative world of the written word, **Jerry Jenkins**, born in 1949 in Kalamazoo, Michigan is best known as the author, along with Tim LaHaye, of the *Left Behind* series of apocalyptic books.

These best-selling novels include *Tribulation*, *Desecration*, *Armageddon* and *Kingdom Come*.

Not only a noted British newspaper columnist but also editor and author, **Simon Jenkins** was born in Birmingham in 1943.

Graduating from St John's College, Oxford with a degree in politics, philosophy and economics, he entered the world of journalism and from 1976 to 1978 was editor of the *London Evening Standard* and then political editor of the *Economist*.

Editor of *The Times* from 1990 to 1992, he now works as a columnist for a number of newspapers and periodicals.

Married from 1981 to 2008 to the American actress Gayle Hunnicut and appointed chairman of the National Trust in 2008, he is the author of a number of books that include his 1979 *Newspapers: The Power and the Money* and the 2011 *A Short History of England*.

Named in 1988 as the *What the Papers Say* Journalist of the Year, he was awarded a knighthood in 2004 for services to journalism.

From the written word to the world of music, **Katherine Jenkins** is the Welsh mezzo-soprano born in Neath in 1980.

The internationally acclaimed performer of not only operatic arias but also popular songs, music theatre and hymns, she studied at the Royal Academy of Music and Drama, London, before first coming to attention when she sang in Westminster Cathedral in 2003 in honour of Pope John Paul II's silver jubilee.

Between 2004 and 2008, no fewer than seven of her albums – including *Premiere*, *Living a Dream* and *From the Heart* – reached number one in the UK classical chart, while her 2007 album *Rejoice* reached number three in the UK pop album charts.

Born in 1933 in Friar's Point, Mississippi, Harold Lloyd Jenkins was the best-selling American country, rhythm and blues, rock and roll and pop singer better known by his stage name of **Conway Twitty**.

It was after deciding that his real name was not 'marketable' enough that, after looking at a road map of the United States he spotted 'Conway', in Arkansas and 'Twitty' in Texas – and it was through this that he chose the name with which he would become famous.

Inspired by the early songs of Elvis Presley, he began writing and performing his own songs and was signed to MGM Records in 1958.

A string of hit songs followed, including *Lonely Blue Boy* – also recorded by Elvis for the film *King Creole* – *Next in Line*, the 1970 *Hello Darlin'*, the 1971 duet with Loretta Lynn *After the Fire is Gone* and the 1975 *Feelins*.

He died in 1996, the recipient of a number of honours and awards that include induction into the Rockabilly, Country Music and Delta Music halls of fame.

In contemporary folk music, **Ella Jenkins**, born in St Louis, Missouri in 1924 and known as "The First Lady of the Children's Folk Song", is the recipient of honours and awards that include a 2004 Grammy Association Lifetime Achievement Award.

This is in recognition of best-selling albums that include her 1966 *You'll Sing a Song and I'll Sing a Song*, the 1970 *Rhythms of Childhood* and the 1981 *I Know the Colors of the Rainbow*.

One bearer of the proud name of Jenkins with a rather unusual claim to musical fame was the American amateur operatic singer **Florence Foster Jenkins**, born in 1868 in Wilkes-Barre, Pennsylvania.

She proved immensely popular with opera lovers – but unfortunately for the wrong reasons.

Audiences flocked to her performances

because, despite her own conviction of her greatness, she was noted and ridiculed for her lack of rhythm, pitch, tone and pronunciation.

Blithely unaware of this – or at least simply choosing to totally ignore it – she compared herself favourably to renowned sopranos of the day, and it was through a substantial sum of money she inherited from her father that she was able to indulge her passion and continue on her sadly deluded way.

But, in addition to ridiculing her, audiences also warmed to her and, at the age of 76, it was because of public demand that she was persuaded to come out of 'retirement' in October of 1944 to deliver a sell-out performance at Carnegie Hall, New York.

Still convinced of her greatness as an opera singer, she died only a month later.